BAD BOYS
FINI$H RICH

THE WORLD'S MOST DANGEROUS
LIFE & ENTRPRENURSHIP
COURSE

Ray Bolden

The book you are about to read is based on the experience of its author, Ray Bolden as well as information he has read or come in contact with. Mr. Bolden does not hold any legal, accounting, or college degrees nor does he or has he ever held a securities license.

Disclaimer
This publication is designed to provide accurate and authoritative information in regard to the subject matter covered. It is sold with the understanding that neither the author nor the publisher is engaged in rendering legal, investment, accounting or other professional advice. Any actions with regard to the information contained in this book should be undertaken only with the advice and counsel of a trained legal professional. If legal advice or other expert assistance is required, the services of a competent professional person should be sought.

The entire project is underwritten by the author. His views and interpretations of the findings may not necessarily be the same as those of the organizations that market the brands that are mentioned in this work.

ISBN-13: 978-0692415849 (Bold Ambition Worldwide, LLC)
ISBN-10: 069241584X

Praise For
BAD BOYS FINI$H RICH

"Thank you from the bottom of my heart. You didn't disappoint and I am happy I found you. I love the direction and the hopeful feeling I am experiencing."
—ERIC, CHICAGO, IL

"This course blew my mind! I'm half way through the workbook and I can't get enough. My attitude toward life has changed. Your book helped me discover strengths I never thought existed, and I have a whole new attitude towards everything."
—WILLIAM, RICHMOND, VA

"I was worried to even open the box, but once I saw the finished product, I was excited. What a book. A masterpiece! Bad Boys Finish Rich helped me understand that it is totally up to me. I can honestly say it saved my life."
—CURTIS, SAN JOSE, CA

"I just wanted to send a quick email to say thanks. I was ready for something different and this course provides a shining light on a better path for me and others to follow."
—ADRIANO, BROOKLYN, NY

"Hi Ray, my name is Chantel. Your book is so amazingly right. The questions and the observations took my breath away. You dove deep into aspects of pain, confusion and fear and I was deeply moved. Thanks."
—CHANTEL, ATLANTA

Dedication

This is dedicated to everyone who feels stuck or trapped. A better way of life is available to you. Go get it!

Table of Contents

Preface 9

Course Objectives 11

*A Different Kind of Education
From A Different Kind of Role Model* 17

PART ONE: Wealth Venture Facilitation

Unlearning & Re-Education 25

Bank on Yourself 33

There Is Only One Way that
You Will Become Rich & Powerful 41

PART TWO: Business Enterprise Option

Create Your Own Game
Within The Game 51

Stop Living Within Your Means
To Escape The Rat Race 63

Own the Team; Don't
Just Play The Game 73

A New Breed Of Rich People 81

Preface

At this very moment, tens of millions of people are looking for new opportunities. An entire generation is realizing that there must be more to life than working themselves to death. People around the world are unsure about how to cope with the changes they're experiencing in both their personal and professional lives. They don't know what to do, and they don't know where to turn for help. They feel lost amidst all the uncertainty, unsure of how to find their place or their potential. Their uncertainty has led to caution and pause that is preventing them from progress. Adopting the *BAD BOYS FINI$H RICH* principles and a more relaxed and carefree attitude will do wonders for the overall well-being of these people. If you dare to follow these principles you can become more creative, more insightful, more productive, wealthier and happier all by being a bad boy or bad girl and enjoying life more.

I don't claim to be an expert or guru, or to have all the answers. My mission is to give you ideas, information, and strategies that can advance you forward in life and entrepreneurship and improve the quality of your life for the rest of your life. The material that follows is derived from my own success, failure and personal experience and is meant to supplement your desire to be successful, but it's not about what I do, it's about what I can help you to do. In this course, you'll find it loaded with my personal trainings, each separated into bite size portions. Please open your mind as you read and take only what you feel you need. I have learned how to make money from successful ideas and even profit from those ventures that don't go as planned so I hope you will use this course as a textbook; which means you will read it many times and refer back to it as your financial intelligence grows. Ambition is the first ingredient needed to be successful and knowledge is the second. When you finish this course, you will be ready for the third most crucial piece of the financial puzzle: Action!

It is my firm belief that any path you choose is the correct one for you. The only difference between paths is the ambition and action we take to arrive at our destination.

This business model provides a vehicle for you to replicate and produces insight needed to create and sustain wealth and successfully take control of your financial destiny. My website can be located at:

www.badboysfinishrich.com

For years the rich have passed wealth secrets down from generation to generation. I have a proven track record demonstrating my ability to create and build money-making opportunities from the idea stage to profitable ventures so my goal is to educate, inspire and encourage you to smartly think differently about success, money and financial intelligence. In this course, I will explain to you what I have done and still do to live my dreams as a self-made entrepreneur. This course offers no abstract theories or suggested experiments.

What you'll find are the real world strategies I have developed and personally use. This course is intended for anyone who has a dream but doesn't know how to put it into action. I believe that if you can show people how they can accomplish a desired goal, they will motivate themselves. By the time you're done with this course, you will feel pride, joy and a sense of accomplishment few ever experience and you will have a clear understanding of a fundamental, profound truth that *"you can do it too!"* Lastly, I value your feedback. If you would like to provide a testimonial or if you simply want to say hello to me and my staff just shoot an email to: admin@badboysfinishrich.com. I'm committed to helping you become successful. Congratulations on beginning your journey to becoming richer than you ever dreamed possible.

Course Objectives

The foundation of what I do is serving others so my primary objective is to teach you to be successful in your own way, and to teach you how to make the most amount of money in the least amount of time. We will do this with the least amount of effort and risk by combining mindset training with financial, business and direct sales education and strategies. The concepts you will learn are unconventional and require a different mode of thinking than what you are used to. To fully comprehend the concepts, you must have the correct mindset. Before you can learn to do, you must first learn what not to do. Not everything will apply to your circumstances, speak specifically to your needs or appeal to your lifestyle, but I'm confident that many of my strategies will work or at the very least serve as inspiration for you to come up with your own formula for success and creative financial solutions. The basic principles are universal. You have invested valuable time and money to learn this material. If you pay attention and absorb the information, you will possess specialized knowledge and strategies that very few people possess. It is your duty to use the information to better your life and the lives of those you care about. Study and review the material as many times as necessary until you have a firm grasp of the concepts. Determine your strengths and weaknesses, and focus on improving your weaknesses with more education and practice.

Stop chasing the next great thing. You've found it! Now learn it and get good at it. Spend your time and money learning things that enhance the core competencies required to master these concepts. If you enjoy great success and profits as a result of this course, I ask only two things of you: 1. Give something back. Donate your time, money or expertise to others who are less fortunate and 2. Tell me about your success! Send me a testimonial and let me know what you accomplished, so that your story can inspire others. I have divided the strategies within this course into two parts that you must learn to master: Wealth Venture Facilitation (WVF) and Business Enterprise Option (BEO). These are by far the two strategies that afford you the best chance of becoming successful, being profitable and learning to build wealth.

WVF is unlearning old behavior models, and breaking free from learned helplessness. It is the process of examining and altering your belief systems, thoughts and values and accepting responsibility for your own creation through self -reliance.

The proven ways to get rich are through the ownership of stocks, real estate and businesses. BEO is determining what side of money you will operate from, putting yourself in a unique position to understand the American Dream and all its possibilities, then creating your own game within the game. This entire course comes down to one thing: *OWNERSHIP*! Owners have power and control. Plain and simple: It's about changing the way that you think. To do this successfully, you must be open-minded, willing to question what you've been taught and thoroughly examine how you see, think and behave regarding matters of wealth and success. This is a course on how to free yourself so buckle up and get ready for a wild ride.

Bad Boy
Function: Noun

1. Someone who follows his own path.
2. Someone who takes risks and creates his own rules.
3. Someone who predicts his own future by creating it.
4. Someone who practices positive, productive self- reliance.
5. Someone who lives outside of the social norm because he does what he wants when he wants.

FINI$H RICH!

"I'm not a businessman. I am a business, man."

~ Jay-Z

Introduction

A DIFFERENT KIND OF EDUCATION FROM A DIFFERENT KIND OF ROLE MODEL

You don't need a college education to become self-made, be successful or even make millions? It's my experience as well as others experiences that have demonstrated over and over that you can become self- made with or without a formal education. Don't get me wrong, this is not an anti-college course. It is a real-life education experience; One that is based on actual life and business strategies. No disrespect to all the educators out there, but this course will not focus on the educational fundamentals of scholastic education, the education that teaches you how to read, write and do arithmetic. Or professional education, the education that teaches you the skill to work for money, such as learning to be a doctor, lawyer, plumber, secretary, electrician or teacher.

Let's make one thing clear before we go any further. It's not an accident that you are here. You're here because you want to be rich. You want money, a big house, and luxury cars and want the freedom to enjoy them. So rather than the same old education you have been receiving, education that teaches you to survive instead of thrive, perform unrewarding 9 to 5 jobs, become complacent, repetitive and monotonous and try to plan for retirement; we will focus on success education: The education that teaches you how to free yourself from societal mediocrity. And financial education: The education that teaches you how to have money work hard for you.

I'm here to let you know that there is nothing wrong with that burning desire that you have for wealth and success. There's nothing to be ashamed of. The question is, "how do you turn that desire into reality?" To answer this question, I'm going to share with you simple yet profound knowledge of what makes the difference in the quality of people's lives, what gives someone a competitive edge and why some people rise above all the challenges and become so much more. I have read damn near every book ever published on wealth and success, but what I found was that it only frustrated me. The information I obtained wasn't feeding me. I wasn't fulfilled. So what do I do? I'm still trying to figure out my life, trying to discover who I really am.

I made a decision about how I was going to live my life and during my pursuit of success, I discovered that it wasn't what I was doing but who I wanted to become that makes all the difference. My research, resources and failed attempts provided everything I needed to create an extraordinary quality of life. I've studied, researched, listened, pondered and questioned what works why and how and I recognize that there are millions of others just like me who want to be rich, but don't know how, who are also frustrated by information that's not feeding them. So, the key to my own success is to share what I have learned, provide a different kind of education and be a different kind of role model.

I realized the purpose of the whole experience wasn't just about creating wealth and success; it was about deepening a relationship with myself. That experience changed my life and through simple interactions, I clearly see the dynamics that are required to succeed. I want to help people understand what it takes to be successful, so the concepts of this course defy most rules and nullify the image of ideal behavior. Success is a subject I take very seriously, so I'm going to teach you something that scares the hell out of most people... *"How to own and control your own life."*

If you are stagnant in your job or are experiencing a mediocre lifestyle, then it's time for you to take action and face the reality that society is consciously and consistently playing mind games with you. We have to reprogram our minds.

In order to succeed, you need to hear the truth. So my goal is to provide real information to people who really want to be successful. Most people avoid truth and ignore and struggle against the inevitable who only leads to continued failures, unhappiness and mediocrity. I want to help you see that you were born for better than this and you are meant to live at a higher level than you are currently. Too many people settle for mediocrity. It's time to rise higher. The question isn't: "What do you have to do to live life at a higher level?" Your answer is "how great do you want to be"? So what does that mean? It means you have to look inside yourself and discover your priceless seeds of greatness then unlock that greatness and allow it to take you to places that you never dreamed possible.

I have experienced this first hand in my life and finding the answer to this question has shaped me and continues to keep me expecting great things in my life, my family and my career. This would be the end of the story except one day an extraordinary event took place. I discovered that I am a brand... A mini-conglomerate. Like Coke, Microsoft and Wal- Mart. Who I am is a business. Negotiating my terms, selling myself and building the worth of my stock. Sometimes I offer discounts but I never reduce the quality of who I am or the benefit of what you will receive from me. I am a mogul; successfully operating the various corporations of me... the parent company.

To totally control my destiny, I had to create it and not search for it in the chaos that doesn't represent me. I had to look into myself not for who it is that I am but for how great I wanted to be. I freed myself from who society tells me I am supposed to be. How many of you are living out your dreams? Most of you are automatically living out society's programs and expectations for you, because that's what you are told to do. The world has lead us to believe that success is out of reach for most of us and only achieved by a select few... the ones who so-called know the secret code. This is exactly the kind of upside down thinking that has caused many of you to lose sight of your dreams.

So, to truly see the kind of results you want, it's imperative that you understand the following principles: Your knowledge of how to get rich sucks and no one is coming to save you. There's only way you will become rich and powerful and that's to create your own game within the game. You must learn to stop living within your means to escape the rat race and learn to own the team; don't just play the game. And within these principles are the following underlying messages.

1. You are either free or you are a slave... there is no in between.
2. The only way to win is to make your own rules.
3. You have to help as many other people as you can.
4. Stop looking for validation.
5. Fuck the critics.
6. Never, ever, ever give up

I have to warn you, practicing these principles could be a potentially life-changing process. It's up to you. Practicing these principles will take you deeper into self- discovery and raise you to a higher level of living. I'll help you to see where you are, where you have been and where you are going. And as we grow together, I'm hoping to help you look inside yourself and ask yourself "Did I ever think that I would be this rich?"

Success is based on sharing and the principles I want to share with you were derived from the struggles and experiences that have transformed me over a considerable period of time. This course is a wide compilation of incredibly fascinating stories laced with life principles and truth; Strong foundations on which much of what I do today is built. If you open your mind and absorb just a small portion of the truth I'm going to share with you, it won't be long before you'll find the success you've always been after. Once you learn the truth and utilize the business opportunity available to you, you will be able to begin living the life you desire.

PART ONE

WEALTH VENTURE FACILITATION

FINI$H RICH!

"If you can control a man's thinking, you don't have to worry about his actions. If you can determine what a man thinks you do not have worry about what he will do. If you can make a man believe that he is inferior, you don't have to compel him to seek an inferior status, he will do so without being told. And if you can make a man believe that he is justly an outcast, you don't have to order him to the back door, he will go to the back door on his own. And if there is no back door, the very nature of the man will demand that you build one."

~ Dr. Carter G. Woodson

Chapter One

UNLEARNING & RE-EDUCATION

(Your knowledge of how to get rich SUCKS!)

There is a good reason why you haven't grasped the fundamentals of getting rich. While schools in America offer classes in various subjects, very few give students a chance to learn simple financial literacy. In fact only fourteen states require schools to offer a consumer education program that includes personal finance. The concept of school has you believing that you lack the knowledge to move ahead. This puts you in a position to lack self confidence in dealing with money or feel insecure financially despite your education? Not surprisingly, the result is that according to one report, basic financial literacy is declining. You have been taught how to earn an income yet you are among millions who do not know how to accumulate wealth. Sadly, a large number of us today desperately want something different in our lives and unfortunately, many people feel like they are trapped in circumstances caused by lack of education, family, upbringing or their environment.

Most of us are taught old behavior models and our point of view on money was inherited. Money was never discussed at home and we were never taught how to get to the other side of money. Sadly, many of us are taught to be satisfied with the status quo. According to respected speaker, teacher and trainer Brian Tracy, "The average person has grown up in a family where he or she has never met or known someone who is wealthy. It never occurs to people that they can become rich. And if it never occurs to you, then you will never take any of the steps to make it a reality. You can grow up and become a fully mature adult in our society without it ever occurring to you that it's just as possible for you to become wealthy as it is for anyone else." Ask most hardworking people how things are going for them and you will hear stories of sixty- to- seventy hour weeks with no time for rest. Even the most affluent people who work at corporations are trapped by unfulfilling lifestyles that their big titles have provided. The result is most individuals are in a state of unconsciousness or self- denial about how their lives are out of sync with their deepest values and beliefs. Entrepreneur, best-selling author and CEO of Operation Hope John Bryant says, "Most of who we are as adults is somehow directly connected to our childhood." So who are you? What great business secrets have been passed down to you? What have you learned about money that can make you successful? Or what lessons about money that you learned from your family are holding you back? How did you end up where you are when you'd prefer to be rich? At some point in your life, you came to the crossroads marked "rich" or "poor" and you chose a way of life. Do you remember who or what influenced you to make that very important quality-of-life decision? Someone you trusted influenced your thinking in a way that had you deciding, "I can't afford it", "That idea will never work" "I'll never be rich" or "I can't do that." Whatever you used as a basis for that decision, it's time to break the core conditioning most of us have learned at home and at school. You can walk away from your experiences and pretend they never happened or you can make them the best experiences of your life.

BOLD AND BRANDED AT BIRTH

When I was young, I inherited my point of view on money. I am Willis Bolden's son. His influence on me was powerful. This course would never have been written if it weren't for him. His story and his choices in life inspired me and changed my life. To tell his story, I need to start at the end. When I was eleven years old, my father died at the age of fifty-one, of hypertension and as far as I know, alcohol related illnesses. He lived his life like most men of his generation; an honest, hardworking family man, but along the way, he became a broken man. He stood for integrity and excellence; and then all of a sudden, he didn't. The psychological impact of all his issues ended up getting the best of him. He worked for Eastern Airlines as a sky cap for twenty- seven years but was fired after being given the opportunity to attend rehab for alcoholism twice.

After continuous efforts to fix their marriage and get him help, he and my mother divorced leaving my mom with five kids to rise and very little money. Now before you think that I blame my father for anything, let me set the record straight: My father's life was his own and the decisions he made were his own. My father's story is a sad story, but remember, I started from the end. His life was also one to be celebrated. He lived life at its highest level his way, and on his terms. My dad was middle class, but his attitude about life was among the elite. Thanks to my father, it was instilled in me to have confidence, ambition and an appreciation for the finer things in life. His was an extraordinary life filled with foundation building events and influential lessons on life, money and entrepreneurship. Allow me to take a moment to share some of them with you. Because of old behavior models, money was never discussed in my family, but whenever me and my brother and sisters would ask my father for money he had a saying, "Don't be in such a hurry to give your money back to the White man." Now for many of you, my father's words may come across as racist or some form of reverse discrimination, but, please take into account that my father lived through a time when racism and second class citizenship for Black men was the law of the land. As a kid, I had no idea what his words meant but I now realize that this was his way of somehow telling me and my brother and sisters to be self- sufficient. He never spoke those direct words but this is a lesson that I have come to understand as a key ingredient for self-made entrepreneurship.

The key to this saying are the words "give your money back." It doesn't matter what color the person is you are giving your money to, the real lesson is that you are giving your money to someone else when it's you who should be getting paid. We'll discuss this in detail in a later chapter. Lesson two of my father's sad but extraordinary life is one of a display of power of sorts; and the number one ingredient needed to become self-made and succeed as an entrepreneur: confidence. It would not have mattered if the President of the United States Barak Obama, himself came to visit, my father would have opened the door and invited him in while standing there in his underwear. Let me paint a picture for you. Fruit of the Loom Tighty-whitey's, the t-shirt tucked into his underwear, black dress socks and black dress shoes. No he wasn't drinking nor would he be drunk. It was simple; his house, his rules.

So at this point you are asking what does this have to do with you and becoming self-made. The lesson is the look of extreme confidence on my father's face that said, "I dare you to ask me why I don't have any clothes on." No shame, no apprehension, just in your face extreme confidence. Although he never taught me how to get to the other side of money, the side where prominent CEO's, Wall Street Tycoons and Business Moguls dwell, without ever realizing it and without really meaning to, my father inspired me to think positive, think big and dream big. We tend to see ourselves and the solutions to our predicament through the eyes of the person or people who influence the way we think. Some of these influences can be negative, but it is directly within our control to navigate through those negative circumstances and unlearn old behavior models. It's up to us to re-educate ourselves and turn them into some kind of advantage to ensure that negative influences are executed positively to the fullest and that no opportunity to succeed is left on the table. Growing up, my surroundings constantly bombarded me with evidence of what it was like to be poor and have no power. The thing I noticed early on was that many people expressed real satisfaction with the status quo. This was a noticeable conflict for me. Most of us have more options than we think we have. Why do people assume they have no power when they have multiple solutions? So often it happens that we live our lives in chains because we don't know we have the key.

Many people think you can only succeed through scholastic education. I have many friends who have this point of view but, education can be adapted to anything. You have to be willing to adapt and this needs to be a part of your strategy. I don't care how many college and post-graduate degrees you've got, learning how to be rich and successful

28

boils down to how you see yourself and how much you love and value yourself. Too many people are willing to stay on the surface of their lives by accepting what their upbringing, their environment and their culture dictate regarding who they are and what they should do then wonder why they struggle financially. You simply cannot play the game of wealth with that mind-set. We have done this for so long that we do not question whether or not our perceptions of reality are accurate. What we've learned and what we've been taught can be distorted. It is not always reality. So when things don't go according to plan even though you are coloring inside the lines, you start to increasingly sense that something is wrong and question whether or not you are on the right road. You can't learn to be rich if you don't know who you are. If your goal is to be a self-made millionaire and you're starting from ground zero, Lesson One in BAD BOYS FINI$H RICH is to unlearn old behavior models, and break free from learned helplessness. To do that, you have to examine how you see, think and behave regarding matters of wealth and success. Author Robert Kiyosaki says, "A person is limited only to his or her reality of what is possible financially. Nothing changes until that person's reality changes. And a person's financial reality will not change until he or she is willing to go beyond the fears and doubts of his or her own self-imposed limits." So before we go any further, now would be a good time to examine why you are where you are. This requires a personal audit, a comparison of your assets and liabilities to determine your net character worth.

The following exercise is just one of several you will encounter within this course. If you attempt all them you will get more out of the content. Actual worksheets can be found in the Appendix section of your *BAD BOYS FINI$H RICH* study guide.

"BAD BOY'S FINISH RICH" – EXERCISE APPENDIX-A

Please take a few minutes, sit back in your chair, breathe deeply and consider the questions below. The purpose of this exercise is to measure who or what is holding you back. Read each question carefully and write down your answer in the space provided before moving on to the next question.

What did you learn from your family that has helped you become financially successful?

Do you feel trapped because of the way your parents raised you to think about money?

What old sayings come to mind when you think about money?

What did you learn from school that has held you back financially?

What did you learn from school that has helped you become financially successful?

What have you learned from your own or someone else's financial success?

What lessons that you learned (from any source) have you applied to your life?

Why do you expect so little of yourself?

Why do you give up your power so easily?

You are where you are and what you are because of your own choices and decisions. What should you change?

FINI$H RICH!

"Nobody can give you freedom. nobody can give you equality or justice or anything. If you're a man, you take it."

~ Malcolm X

Chapter Two

BANK ON YOURSELF

(No one is coming to save you)

Powerlessness is a tremendous motivator to pursue power... financial power. But nothing comes easy, it's a daily battle. Many of you have lost interest in climbing the corporate ladder and absolutely detest being programmed into becoming something you don't want to be anymore. And for those of you not in corporate America but simply working at a job that you hate; you don't have to do much to live a mediocre life.

If that's what you wanted, you wouldn't be taking this course. When it comes to having a successful life, the two options seem to be (1) staying within the system and working long and hard hours or (2) dropping out of the system completely to pursue a life of being bad and total leisure. How do you fit into this picture? It's simple, since no one is coming to save you, you have to save yourself. This represents an enormous change for many of you because until now you have simply colored inside the lines. You don't own businesses or invest in real estate; you are simply playing the game. This is a free country; we can be as rich as we want.

IT'S PERSONAL

In the mirror is the person who will become your mentor. They are filled with financial intelligence and their point of view represents the other side of entrepreneurship and money; an elite group that you want to belong to. Your future is filled with building businesses and owning the team; not just playing the game. To expand your reality, you must answer crucial questions. It's not only about education, it's about re-education. Saving yourself begins at a point that many of you may recognize; a point in life many of us have shared, the point of starting with nothing. It is simply changing your mindset from negotiating from a position of weakness to making deals as one among equals. To do that, you have to have an action-orientated system, specifically designed to support and guide you on your way. It will help put you in a wealthier state of mind, give you clarity about who you are, what your aspirations are, and what you need to do to achieve them quickly.

A LEGITIMATE HUSTLE BUT A HUSTLE JUST THE SAME

My story starts the same as many others, with a real life desire to succeed with constraints on time and money. I spent 21 years in the military. I made decent money and played by the rules, but something shifted in my mindset and I lost interest in climbing the military ladder. I wanted to be rich, but I didn't know how. Military personnel are authorized to retire after twenty years of service, so after retiring, I spent approximately four months in corporate America then I quit. That meant that I was only going to have a little money from my retirement check, no job, and no assets. Everybody and I do mean everybody thought that I was crazy, so I had to do a serious reality check. I could choose to be stuck in this spot if I don't make something major happen; or worse, I could choose to go back to the life of mediocrity that I was so desperately trying to get away from. After moving into a new home, one day I received a business opportunity magazine in the mail addressed to the former homeowner. I flipped through it and my curiosity got the best of me. I paid particular interest to an ad about a guy who made $100,000.00 creating little books and selling them from home. I ordered it and studied it over and over again.

Shortly thereafter, I created my own little books and began selling them through the mail. The response was slow, but I continued to follow the tips, tricks and techniques that I learned from his system and sales trickled in. This was enough to get me excited. I started doing research and gained ideas at the bookstore, library and by listening to audio programs. I took those ideas and with a lot of trial and error, started developing my own winning formula and with a little ingenuity and creativity, I adapted this formula to the Internet. No one was coming to save me; so I had to save myself. This allowed me to learn, experience and invent who Ray Bolden was going to become. It was through this internal struggle that the *BAD BOYS FIN$H RICH* brand was born and I created a lifestyle around it. This is where so many of us struggle. Even though we're capable of carving our own path, we still act and feel like we are stuck, waiting for someone else to save us. We continually doubt our ability because we are afraid that we'll fail, so we don't even try. I h o p e this statement will excite indignation from you as most statements that are true, but that you want to deny tend to do. If your life is far from being as satisfying and fulfilling as you would like it to be, you have created this mess in the first place. Ultimately, no one is forcing you to be like everybody else and live a mediocre life. You alone have chosen to do so. This makes you totally responsible for the stress and turmoil that you are bringing into your life and it stems from your willingness to go along with what everybody else is doing.

The key to remember here is that this isn't a plan to get rich quick, it is a plan to do what needs to be done and stop looking for others to meet the desires that only you can meet. Now I could be wrong, you might be comfortable knowing that you are in a large majority of individuals whose lives are mediocre and unfulfilling. It might be easier for you to follow the crowd than to think differently and do things on your own. You don't have to be one of those people. You always have an alternative. For *BAD BOYS who FINI$H RICH*, the key to success is refusing to accept society's definition of success as your own. I have failed miserably many times, but I also achieved success beyond my wildest dreams. One of the hardest struggles is trying to make your mark in life, so although it hasn't been an easy process, the experience has been priceless. Most people wait for others like the company that they work for or the military to take care of them and in a lot of ways they let their jobs dictate who they are. I never had a master plan, I just got fed up one day and decided to do something about it. The alternative is to live a mediocre life, trapped in a safe job (if those even exist anymore) with a mediocre paycheck. Because of age and experience and my growing frustration with being an employee, I began to crave financial freedom. I decided that since no one was going to ask me to join the club, I had to start my own club. This represented an enormous change for me because until then, I had simply colored inside the lines. I got angry. Mad at myself because this is a free country, we can be as rich as we want. I met the man who would become my mentor in the mirror. Although he didn't know it at the time, he was filled with financial intelligence and very well spoken if I say so myself. His point of view represented the other side of entrepreneurship and money; the elite group that I wanted to belong to. Although he was skeptical at first because he was afraid I would quit once I found out how hard it could be, he agreed to teach me what he knew if I would apprentice with him and work for free. Excited and filled with confidence, all I wanted was the opportunity to learn. His future was filled with owning the team, building businesses and investing in what some people call the real estate of the twenty-first century, not just playing the game. He asked me a series of crucial questions that changed my life forever: What did I want out of life? What was my specific goal? How would I get there? And what was my game plan? Because of our association, I have learned more about success from my mentor than I did in school or from the military. I have gained the experience of a lifetime. I have not only become a wiser business person, I have also learned a great deal about creating wealth and success. To quote Robert Kiyosaki, "My reality on how rich a person can become has expanded and my reality on what is possible financially will never be the same."

So I faithfully describe to you the plan that was laid out for me by that man in the mirror and I'm simply relating the process I went through once I knew the direction I wanted my life to take. I encourage you to take that look in the mirror and see who looks back. Be honest and stare yourself down. Even if you see fear, keep looking. Even if you see insecurity, keep looking. Ask the person that you see in the mirror what they see and be prepared to be empowered by their response. Then commit yourself to study and learn how to be who they say you are going to become. To save yourself, I offer the following contract.

"BAD BOYS FINI$H RICH" – EXERCISE APPENDIX-B

BAD BOYS FINI$H RICH Bank On Yourself Contract

To bank on myself, I hereby declare to become successful, healthy, happy and rich!

1. What do you want out of life?_____
2. What is your specific goal? _____
3. How will you get there? _____
4. What is your game plan? _____
5. For the next 12 months I will earn an average of $ _____per day: $ _____ per week; $ _____ per month; $_____ for the next year.
6. I will have saved $ _____ by the end of the 12 months.
7. I will travel to: _____
8. I will drive: _____
9. I will live in a: _____
10. For this increased income and lifestyle, I will serve more people.

All of the above is a part of my Bank on Myself process. With the above intentions expressed in writing, I am beginning to achieve my financial and personal goals. I verify my commitment to the above by fixing my signature hereto.

Signature_____

FINI$H RICH!

"If you are what you say you are, a superstar, then have no fear"

~ Lupe Fiasco

Chapter Three

THERE IS ONLY ONE WAY THAT YOU
WILL BECOME RICH & POWERFUL

(It's the thought that counts)

The average person, (about 85% of us), will retire without sufficient income to live comfortably for the rest of their lives. Because they don't know how, a significant portion of the population has given up on achieving the American Dream. Ironically for most people, the idea of achieving mega-wealth and being super rich isn't even a thought. They've come to accept a life of surviving instead of striving and have been taught to think small, feel inferior and to accept limitations. The truth is, deep down everyone wants to be wealthy. This leads us to a major problem in contemporary society: most people don't know how to truly live so this is your chance to forget the past and seize the day. I beg you to listen carefully to the words of business philosopher Jim Rohm "Let others lead small lives, but not you. Let others leave their future in someone else's hands, but not you." You really do want to live in a mansion, drive exotic cars and travel around the world in private jets. It's nothing to be ashamed of. On the contrary, it's a goal worthy of your pursuit every minute of every day. You just have to make different choices and take action on those choices. There's an anonymous quote that says "the greatest waste in the world is the difference between who we are and what we could've become", so hear me loud and clear. Decide what you want, focus single- mindedly on your objective and make becoming who you are capable of becoming a priority in your life. Let me explain.

Since you don't know how to become rich, you have got to teach yourself to think like *BAD BOYS who FINI$H RICH* think. So let's start by talking about what all *BAD BOYS who FINI$H RICH* have in

41

common.   Typically *BAD BOYS who FINI$H RICH have* a more positive mindset than most others. They sincerely believe that they deserve the best of the best and that even their wildest dreams can come true. They have an unshakable belief that miracles do happen, but they also understand that they have to make them happen. *BAD BOYS who FINI$H RICH* read a minimum of two books per month: Mostly history, biographies and money management.   Mention the word problem to a BAD BOY who FINI$HES RICH and he or she will only hear the term opportunity. BAD BOYS who FINI$H RICH break away from the crowd and ignore conventional wisdom with courage and conviction because being bad is a mind-set and perspective. It's a way of looking at the world. Instead of seeing it for what it is, it is looking at it for what it could be.

SUCCESS REDEFINED

Seven out of ten adults polled recently said that they don't earn enough money to live the kind of life that they want to live and seven out of ten say that getting rich is their most important goal in life. That's why you are here.   You are tired of living on somebody else's terms, somebody else's schedule and under financial restraint. You believe that there is much more to you than what others see, yet you are pissed off because you have no idea or even the slightest clue what you could do to be able to create the lifestyle you really want to live.

Alright, I admit it; it was me who felt this way. I was pissed off because the status quo wasn't working for me. At least not what I felt met my standard. I wanted a better life than the one I had. Now, don't get me wrong, I already had a 3000 Sq. ft. home, a sports car and a luxury SUV, but my goal was freedom. Was I scared? Of course I was! But that's no excuse for inaction. To be happy, I had to leave my comfort zone. I got tired of watching other people live in multi-million dollar homes, drive Ferrari's, Bentleys and travel in   Private Jets. I was a little envious, not jealous, just a little envious… "What the hell do these people do? And "how did they learn to get rich? This is a question that constantly haunts all of us. Right now, you might be better off than I was or worse, but I was in a place where I wanted to change everything. I wanted something better with an emphasis on ownership and control in whatever I decided to do. I didn't want any limitations on what I thought I could earn. I wanted to be my own boss. Why should I brand someone else's company when I can brand my own? I wanted my name on the letterhead and I was determined to place the words Ray Bolden and Capitalist in the same sentence. I vowed that entrepreneurship held the key to my future and that I would be the owner because I realized that this was the key to my longevity and building generational wealth. I definitely didn't know what I was getting into, but I was excited about it.

You're taking this course because you want to be rich, but simply wanting to be rich won't get it for you. There's a bigger issue at stake.
One of the things I learned quickly is that before you can be rich, you have to make becoming rich your intention. The human mind can be accommodating. It can usually find justification for the decisions that it makes so my hope is that you'll see that there is no magic secret to getting rich. Instead, there is focus, dedication, creativity and sacrifice. Putting all these solutions into action is absolutely free. You are at a point in history when the opportunity for moving ahead has never been greater and you can seize this moment by taking charge of your own reprogramming. If you're caught up in negative thinking or hating the world for the circumstances of your life, you are not going to get anywhere. You have to start thinking positively about your resources for improving your life and believe that you can make it happen. *BAD BOYS who FINI$H RICH* are ambitious self-starters who possess a deep need for internal control of their lives. Think about it: if you do the same thing everyone else around you is doing, where is it going to get you? It will get you the same place it is getting them, right? If you don't like the results your family, friends, or co-workers are getting with their life, then go in the opposite direction!

43

BAD BOYS who FINI$H RICH understand that if you want to be rich, you must study the acquisition of wealth. Most importantly, *BAD BOYS who FINI$H RICH* make financial literacy a priority by studying and absorbing new information. Your money should be paying you back. Instead of spending your life working hard for the dollar, find a way to make your dollars do some of the work for you. If you want to be a *BAD BOY* who *FINI$HES RICH*, you need to think rich. It's not what you have to do, first it's how you think.

THE MINDSET THAT GOVERNS THE THINKING OF BAD BOYS WHO FINI$H RICH

- ✓ BAD BOYS who FINI$H RICH rewrite the rules!
- ✓ BAD BOYS who FINI$H RICH work for profits not wages!
- ✓ BAD BOYS who FINI$H RICH spend money to make money!
- ✓ BAD BOYS who FINI$H RICH cut a path where none existed before!
- ✓ BAD BOYS who FINI$H RICH plan their work and work their plan!
- ✓ BAD BOYS who FINI$H RICH transfer their knowledge into power!
- ✓ BAD BOYS who FINI$H RICH make money while others make excuses!
- ✓ BAD BOYS who FINI$H RICH not only take the initiative, they take charge!
- ✓ BAD BOYS who FINI$H RICH play to win with confidence and commitment!
- ✓ BAD BOYS who FINI$H RICH not only think outside the box, they create the box!
- ✓ BAD BOYS who FINI$H RICH break the rules and thrive on the process of change!
- ✓ BAD BOYS who FINI$H RICH walk and conduct their business with a sense of purpose!

- ✓ BAD BOYS who FINI$H RICH not only see things as they could be, but as they insist that they be!
- ✓ BAD BOYS who FINI$H RICH believe that sooner or later they are going to be successful!
- ✓ BAD BOYS who FINI$H RICH know that they have something unique and valuable to offer!
- ✓ BAD BOYS who FINI$H operate in a constant state of motion, driven by a sense of urgency!
- ✓ BAD BOYS who FINI$H RICH stand their ground and push hard even when the world opposes!
- ✓ BAD BOYS who FINI$H RICH lift their heads above the crowds because they are independent and self-reliant!
- ✓ BAD BOYS who FINI$H RICH not only want to corner the market; they want to change the game!
- ✓ BAD BOYS who FINI$H RICH think about what is to come and set clear goals with intention and purpose!
- ✓ BAD BOYS who FINI$H RICH are always learning, forever absorbing information from every possible source and at every opportunity!
- ✓ BAD BOYS who FINI$H RICH refuse to entertain, dwell on or discuss the likelihood of failure. The concept of failure never occurs to them!

BAD BOYS FINI$H RICH is a habit and an attitude! To change what you have you will need to change your intention. Start with your attitude, mindset and beliefs. You have the power to change the quality of your life. You've been w anting to change, but if it hasn't happened, it's because the intention was missing. How do I know that? Because "Intention Always = Results.

"BAD BOYS FINI$H RICH" – EXERCISE APPENDIX-C

Grab a pen and put it in your left palm. Now, try to pick up your pen with your right hand...

You picked it up!

I didn't say "Pick it up;" I said, "Try to pick it up." The point of this exercise is that you can't try to do anything. You either do it or you don't. Once you accept this truth as a basic reality of life, you'll begin to see that it's easy to do what *BAD BOYS who FINI$H RICH* do if you learn to think like *BAD BOYS who FINI$H RICH* think. I tried is just an excuse for choosing not to do what you say you want to do. What's been missing is your willingness and your intention to change your life. You have to go beyond just wanting something and get to the point of seriously making what you want your intention.

PART TWO

BUSINESS ENTERPRISE OPTION

FINI$H RICH!

"When I control the rules of the game, I always win; especially when I'm the only one who knows the rules."

~ Ray Bolden

Chapter Four

CREATE YOUR OWN GAME WITHIN THE GAME

(You are either free or you are a slave)

The American Heritage Dictionary defines slavery as:

1. The state of one bound in servitude as the property of a slaveholder or household.
2. The condition of being subject to a specified influence.
3. The state of being under control of another person.

L et me explain the concept of slavery as it relates to *"BAD BOYS FINI$H RICH."* Slavery is not a physical state but a mental state. Anyone who carries the notion that they lack the ability to create their own game within the game or feels as if they must rely upon the decisions and influence of others who hold the key to their financial future is still a slave. This sort of claim invites skepticism and explanations and excuses from the systematic mass of people who have no power or control. Society has successfully created the overwhelmingly popular, inaccurate perception that you are incapable of creating your own economic reality. It's unfortunate but true that many of us allow ourselves to believe this and therefore allow ourselves to continually play someone else's game and continually lose. It is imperative that you free yourself from this form of mental slavery that prevents you from achieving economic independence. Andrew Young said it best when he said, "To live in a system of free enterprise and yet not understand the rules of free enterprise, that's the definition of slavery." Capitalism works and everyone has the potential to become a millionaire. However, because of the competitive nature of capitalism everyone is not forced to live the same lifestyle. You have to choose. Which group do you want to join? Do you want to own or rent your life? People with less ambition and old behavior models are left with crumbs; a smaller piece of the pie. Everybody's making money on transactions except you. This entire course comes down to *OWNERSHIP & FREEDOM*! Owners have power and control. Renters or leasers are powerless.

MAKING THE BEST CHOICES FOR YOU, YOUR LIFE AND YOUR MONEY

There are two types of people in this world: those who are proactive and those who are reactive. Both are blessed to enter a wide-open world of opportunity. The reactive person lives his or her life by responding to opportunity if it ever comes. The proactive person approaches opportunity completely different however. The proactive person lives by preparing for what could occur in advance and making his or her own opportunities. If you want to be free, you can no longer afford to keep responding to your situation. You owe it to yourself to embrace the *"BAD BOYS FINISH RICH"* principles and be proactive in your own game. Which team do you want to play on? The choice is so obvious. Given a clear choice, always choose wealth and opportunity. Choose to own instead of rent your life and then lift others up and give everyone hope and opportunity. Everybody, regardless of what they admit out loud wants to live the life of a millionaire. If they didn't, nobody would play the lottery, or watch "Who Wants To Be a Millionaire?" Getting rich ultimately begins and ends with taking control of yourself. It starts with a very personal decision. It is a very important decision because whichever financial position in life you choose, be it rich, poor or middle class, then everything in your life changes. In her book *A Return to Love* Marianne Williamson put it this w a y , " Our deepest fear is that we are powerful beyond measure. It is our light, not our darkness, that most frightens us. We ask ourselves, who am I to be brilliant, gorgeous, talented, and fabulous? Actually, who are you not to be? Your playing small does not serve the world."

No matter what stage of life you are currently in, you must find a way to create your own game within the game. You are not born self-made, and overnight success almost always requires years of hard work and sacrifice. Achieving wealth and success requires knowledge... financial literacy. You have to learn the right rules. Not just the kind of book smarts you learn at school, because you can graduate from school and be able to quote business philosophy verbatim, but in reality, that's not all that's needed to be successful in life or business. The truth is, you can step back and not play someone else's game, but you have to understand how the game is played, then create your own game within the game.

You have to impose yourself on the situation because only one of you can win. And you have to make sure the game is played according to your objectives so that you don't get caught up in someone else's game plan. The key to your success is relying on the power within yourself rather than something external. This seems obvious when you think about it, but somehow until it's called to our attention; most of us don't realize it. It's imperative that we all become aware of our options so I propose these five steps as starting points toward economic self-interest and creating your own game within the game:

1) Set aside a place at home to reflect, meditate and broaden your understanding of the game you are playing and your role in it. (work, school, military etc.)

2) Rethink the way you look at the game (How have you contributed to the problem? How can you counteract it?)

3) Surround yourself with books, articles and anything that can feed your entrepreneurial and financial curiosity.

4) Diversify your educational consumption with documentaries, educational programs and stories of success, wealth and entrepreneurial growth.

5) Intellectualize and articulate the concept, then demonstrate your commitment through your behavior.

It's not rocket science, but most of us have never been taught these simple yet powerful principles of financial literacy that can turn the direction of our financial energy from cash out to cash in. Some people will be open-minded and decide to try to create their own game within the game, but others will argue with you and try to tell you why what you're doing doesn't make sense. And they'll stay the course even when that course clearly isn't working for them out of fear of taking another route. Even lab rats will go down a dead end path in a maze only once or twice before giving up and trying a different way. You may be shocked to learn how much wealth you are unnecessarily losing by doing things the conventional way. Most of us waste a lifetime wandering down the same blind alley, refusing to even try going in another direction. Please understand this is about a different way to think. It illustrates mind-bending financial principles not taught in business, economics or finance courses, and most people have never even considered it because we've been systematically taught to be afraid of our true greatness and our true potential.

Please believe that there is nothing that you cannot do. Remember, you are the CEO of your life and the possibilities are limitless. The only thing that will limit you is the capacity of your imagination and confidence in your self-worth.

CONFESSIONS OF A
SELF-MADE ENTREPRENEUR

I have a confession to make: I'm a dreamer, a visionary and an independent thinker. I'm not afraid of failing. As a matter of fact, I understand that failing is a natural part of the path to success. Trust me; nothing comes easy, it's a daily battle. I have repeatedly risked everything I have in order to succeed; both in my personal and business lives. I'm like a Bumble Bee. Bumble Bees are aero dynamically unsound. They can't fly. But, Bumble Bees don't know that they are aero dynamically unsound, so they fly anyway. I didn't know that I didn't know what I was doing, so I flew anyway. Many of the businesses I've tried failed even before they got off the ground. I laugh now at how naïve I was back then when I reflect back on some of them. Some of those businesses did very well and the educational experience has been priceless for me.

If I believed everything that I heard from mainstream society and the media regarding who I am who I should be and what was best for me, I would have been in real trouble. Although it has not been an easy process for me, it has been a very exciting one. As I write this course, I have built enough passive income to allow me to work for myself out of my home instead of getting a job. I am in complete control of my time. That in turn creates a vicious cycle meaning more power and more access to wealth and opportunity. Being rich goes hand in hand with ownership and freedom and you can't be truly rich until you own your own life, own your future and have the freedom to make your own decisions.

80% YOU, 20% THEM

Change is hard and it can be scary but the effort is worth it. Every person that improved his or her life made the choice and did something about it. There is no such thing as fear, not to an entrepreneur. Concern yes. Fear No! I realized that I had to change the way I was thinking.

What a lot of people don't understand is that they will be flying high in their profession and feeling like they're part of the family, but they're not a part of the family. They are entirely expendable and there's always a day when you find that out. Let me be blunt and honest: In my own search for economic balance and power I longed for something that spoke directly to my struggle. I have been exposed to literally thousands of financial products, strategies and concepts, many of which were touted as sure bets for growing wealth but after careful investigation most proved to be worthless or even hazardous to my financial health.

To offset this, I started to look at the whole notion of wealth and quality of life in a different way. I was smart, determined, ambitious, and focused and like most people, I wanted to acquire status, money and material things. So I approached everything and I do mean everything from an entrepreneurial perspective. 80% Me, 20% Them! While at work, I gave them a gut-wrenching 20% of all I had but my focus was always, on me, my future and what I could learn, grasp and use from my immediate surroundings. I chose to divest as best I could from anything that didn't empower me at the end of the day and that gave me power to rail against the establishment but live a comfortable and carefree life. It can take a tremendous amount of time for people from the corporate or traditional work world to understand this concept but, you have to have a grand vision of yourself despite your present circumstances that will propel you into action and achievement. I'm living my life now more as the person I am, not as the person I was pretending to be and I have a rebellious streak, openly mocking the corporate establishment while at the same time profiting from it. The world is wide open and money no longer rules my life. Getting away from American consumerism and status competitions allowed me to focus on what mattered.

Success for me is, can I wake up in the morning and feel free? Stuff in and of itself has little value. It's what we do with it that matters. What excites me is starting companies. I am one of those natural entrepreneurs who live to reimagine markets, invent new products and obsessively pursue ideas that sound insane to everyone else but make perfect sense to me. I care about helping people solve their problems and reach their potential and my businesses are based on helping others by providing valuable information that can improve their lives.

While the story of getting rich has become a tired cliché in American culture, it's time to move away from the mediocre dumbed-down information that dominates society and move into real-life practices of creating your own game. My mission is to improve the lives and businesses of those I serve so m y goal is to uplift, encourage and empower a new wave of big thinkers. I want to create more owners. I want to create millionaires. I want you to own a piece of the American Dream, so my goals are aligned with yours. My goal is to encourage success, to empower you to dream big, think big and achieve big. It doesn't matter what your reasons are. I am on your side that's all you need to know. Unfortunately, we live in an immediate gratification society and some people are looking for a quick fix or magic bullet. They want something that they can put under their pillow before they go to sleep and wake up rich in the morning. Well, I'm going to make a very bold statement that I can and will back up in this course: " Creating your own game within the game is a surprisingly simple way to turn the direction of financial energy in your life toward you so that you can jump ahead financially, even if that seems unimaginable to you now." You don't need any advanced skill or specialized knowledge and it only takes imagination to implement and monitor. Although it's not magic, the benefits you get do seem quite magical, but it takes patience and discipline. It was challenging for me as most significant changes in life tend to be but, for those of you who have similar aspirations, I offer the following guidelines: To facilitate your metamorphosis and know that you too can obtain economic supremacy within the context of your current situation, it's time to transform your economic self-interest by being more selective about the information you place in your mind.

This is not about living above your means or keeping up with the Jones'. These steps aim to provide meaningful ways to reconnect with your economic self-interest. It's not about completely abandoning your current practices, but taking the first steps toward overall empowerment.

Exposure to this concept prepared me to be receptive to other wealth building experiences. You will win if you chose to do so. So dream it, see it and do it.

"BAD BOYS FINI\$H RICH" – EXERCISE APPENDIX-D

- Identify how your thinking has created the game you are playing. What should you, or could you change?

- You have the ability to create and win your own game. What do you want to be, have and do?

- How would you play the game if you created the rules?

- How would you measure your success if you created and played your own game?

- What would you do differently with your life if you created the rules?

- What would you do, and how would you spend your time if you knew you were going to win the game you create?

- What is the price you will have to pay in additional work, time and commitment to play the type of game that is important to you?

- Project forward five years and look back to the present. What would have to have happened for you to win your game?

- What one action should you take immediately as the result of your answers to the previous questions?

- List the excuses that are holding you back, then imagine that they have no basis and act accordingly.

- Describe how you will apply the 80% YOU/20% THEM thinking principle to every area of your life.

Never give yourself an excuse to lose. Close all existing exits so that you can never turn back, and have no other alternative but to win.

FINI$H RICH!

"I'm hungry! You can throw me butt-naked in the jungle and I'll come out with a chin-chilla coat, a leopard skin hat and 10lbs heavier from eating them niggas!"

~ Derek Luke as Sean Puffy Combs in the movie "Notorious"

Chapter Five

STOP LIVING WITHIN YOUR MEANS
TO ESCAPE THE RAT RACE

(Make a living with your day job; make your
fortune with what you've got on the side)

As a society, we tend to fall into the financial divide between those with an employee mentality: people who rely on a boss or company to pay their bills, versus those who think of themselves as owners, entrepreneurs, small-business owners, independent contractors and professionals. The difference is owning or renting your life. How much you make and how you do it is only limited by your ability to take control of who you are and who you want to be.

Once I could see the different sides of money, I could no longer buy into the idea of life as an employee. I don't want to come across like some brilliant investment guy and I don't think that I'm smarter than anybody because before I got to this point, I had brain damage like everybody else. And as a matter of fact, I've had my ass handed to me plenty of times. You can ask what kind of psychological or intellectual stuff was behind all this, but the answer is pretty simple: I woke up one day and decided my life needed to change. Along the way, I discovered a new culture of wealth that's vastly different from the way I was taught that money was made, and I found fortunes from sides of money I barely knew existed. To say my mind was blown would be an understatement. Life is full of perpetual frustration and disbelief, and there is always someone else making more money with less work and discipline. The purpose of my journey isn't to take sides in this debate and I haven't set out to condemn sides. Money is a great liberator; it gives us freedom and choice. If I can get people just a little bit more informed then maybe they will concentrate on things that will make their financial situation better and make themselves truly happy.

To allow you to build a better financial and psychological levee to protect you against upcoming financial storms and floods, I offer the following tips.

In his book the *Cashflow Quadrant*, Robert Kiyosaki introduced the Cashflow Quadrant, a trademark of Cashflow Technologies, Inc. The letters in the quadrant simply represent the sides of money that a person generates income from. In his book, he specifies four quadrants:

Side 1: The E quadrant stands for: Employee

Side 2: The S quadrant stands for: Self-Employed

Side 3: The B quadrant stands for: Business Owner

Side 4: The I quadrant stands for: Investor

Within this course, I'll introduce you to a 5th side of money that can act as a bridge to your financial freedom.

SEEING AROUND CORNERS

What I learned in school and in the military made me a professional in Side 1: the "E" (employee) quadrant. I felt secure there with a regular paycheck, allowances, and other benefits. But as I grew older, I also felt like I was running an endless race. I didn't think much of it though, because I was doing what I had always been taught and acting according to the incentives of the system: work for a steady paycheck, benefits and job security.

On Side 1: The E quadrant: No matter what, there's always someone higher than you who gives orders and dictates how much you make. Side2: the "S" (self-employed) quadrant people are professionals who are their own boss. Most of them are well-educated, work-a-day professionals such as doctors, lawyers or accountants, or self-employed consultants, real estate agents, etc. I operate out of the "S" quadrant as a self-publisher allowing me to serve my clients, tell my story and share my message of self-reliance through books, audio programs and video training sessions. According to Joyce A. Myers, "A #2 pencil and a dream can take you anywhere." I agree completely. Side 2: "S" quadrant people can dictate their income with the work that they put in. I took this path to learn skills that could be used to continue building my businesses. Typically the downside of Side 2: the "S" quadrant is the more successful you become, the less time you will have because you are the boss and the expert who knows your particular craft best. But, how times have changed! My industry is perfect for outsourcing. We live in a free-agent nation so you don't have to have a big team to succeed. With intelligent delegation; virtual assistants and outsourced contractors allow you to outsource your needs on a project-by-project basis.

I've heard it said many times, "If you want to be rich, you need to be a business owner and an investor," which brings me to the next two sides of money.

WEALTH BEGETS POWER, WHICH BEGETS MORE WEALTH

As you move from sides 1 and 2 to sides 3 and 4, the number of entrepreneurs and business owners starts to increase and your entire philosophy of money changes. The people on sides 3 and 4 have one thing in common: their wealth is increasingly linked to financial markets; either through the companies they start and sell or through salaries paid with shares or options. They make their money from salaries, small business or investment returns. Ask a billionaire for his or her financial statement and you'll get a flow chart of interlocking subsidiaries, holding companies, investment funds and foundations. Traditionally, Side 3: the "B" (business owner) quadrant is where you own a system and people work for you. I also operate out of Side 3: the "B" quadrant as owner of BOLD Ambition Worldwide, LLC, and a top-tier direct sales company. Because you can reach so many people and share information and digital products so inexpensively with the worldwide activity of the Internet, today it's possible to build businesses with zero or just a few employees where traditional business standards don't apply. To offset the traditional corporate definitions of a true side 3: "B" quadrant business owner I use associates or affiliates for increased exposure and to increase sales of my products.

Side 4: the "I" (investor) quadrant is where your money works for you even while you sleep. For decades, one of the best ways to become wealthy as an investor was through real estate. Today it is information. To operate out of Side 4: the "I" quadrant and generate additional income streams, I create subscription programs which are just like the magazine business model. Let me show you this concept in motion: If I get just 100 people to pay $97 a month for my subscription program, I Will earn $9,700 per month which equals an astounding $116,000 per year. Even real estate guru Robert Allen claims: "There is a lot more money in the information business than there will ever be in the real estate business." Remember, this is a course about you. If you can create information that helps people solve their problems and market it effectively, you can prosper and generate more wealth than most people can with real estate.

I try to avoid relying on a single source of income to fund my lifestyle and retirement. No matter where you start or how unfair life is, every person who wants to be rich but doesn't know how should make money working for you a part of your retirement portfolio because for most of us wealth is a long distance marathon rather than a sprint.

Your income potential is unlimited on Side 3 and 4, the "B" and "I" sides; you don't necessarily have to work in these quadrants. On the other hand, your time and earning potential are limited on sides 1 and 2 the "E" and "S" quadrants. Why, because traditional education trains us for sides 1 and 2, the "E and S" quadrants; this where we work hard for money. It would be nice at this stage of the course to offer my grand solution, but there is no easy fix. I always turn to my most reliable tool: my gut instinct. I'm not telling you what to do, but at least you have some choices. Take the power and control out of the hands of strangers and chose to take control and ownership yourself. That's how you own your future.

AN ALTERNATIVE
SCHOOL OF THOUGHT

Side 5: the "N" Network marketing quadrant is the average person's best way to become wealthy. Even if you work full-time, you can build a Network marketing career on the side while paying the bills with your full-time pay check. In Network marketing, each person owns their own home-based business. Think of the network marketing business system as a bridge: a bridge that can provide you a path to cross safely from sides 1 & 2 to financial freedom on sides 3 & 4. If your goal is financial independence as an entrepreneur, then Side 5: the "N" Network marketing quadrant offers some of the quickest, low risk ways to achieve it. Network marketing allows people like you and me to make money for the marketing we are already doing every day on websites like Facebook and Twitter.

It's as simple as referring a product. Once you've referred someone to the product, if they like it and want to make money from it for the people they tell about it; when they do, you'll also get paid because you are the one who started this snowball effect of referrals for the product! For a reasonable entry fee, you can buy into an existing business system and immediately start building your own business. Side 5: the "N" Network marketing quadrant is the perfect opportunity for you to learn sales and marketing: the most important function of any business. The headaches of paperwork, processing orders, distribution, accounting and follow-up are almost entirely managed by the network marketing software systems and most of all you are trained on how to successfully market the products. It's like buying a personal franchise. You acquire the rights to a proven system and then your only job is to develop your people. All you need is the ability to follow a simple system and of course the right mind-set to leverage the company's resources. How much time and energy you commit to your Side 5: "N" Network marketing business is completely up to you.

In life, at least twice we reach a point where we consciously decide where we are going regarding our lives and our careers. Obviously, the first time is when we get out on our own and try to make a way for ourselves. The second time we take stock of where we've gotten thus far is around the age of 40. For some of us it may happen sooner but more often than not, at 40 we haven't gotten to where we thought we'd be in terms of health, careers or especially money and this can cause stress or denial which manifests as a mid- life crisis. To explain how a person makes the right choices at these critical points, I'll quote two people here: Niccolo Machiavelli said, "Make mistakes of ambition and develop strength to do bold things not the strength to suffer." Thomas H. Huxley, English biologist; known as Darwin's bulldog said, "It is far better for a man to go wrong in freedom than to go right in chains." These quotes are relevant because they will help you think about the possibilities you probably never knew existed.

The first thing to appreciate about possibilities is that there are 5 sides of money which means there are 5 ways to live your life. Please clearly understand these 5 distinctions before you continue. The challenge is to find out how many different ways you can take money and make more money with it. Most people struggle because they don't have a clue how to do this. Why? Because we just don't know that we can. We think we have to earn and live our lives based on the education we have. We are taught by our side 1 & 2 mentors that we can only dream about what we can achieve then we have to compete for growth within this limited space. Interestingly, these are completely baseless ideals for people on sides 3, 4 & 5. By my own standards, I can say that I live a great life and I can honestly say that I created it for myself. I realized that only I have control over what side of money I create my lifestyle from and I don't let anybody tell me what to do. My attitude is always positive, I'm not afraid to take risks and

I work hard to create my own opportunities. The secret to freedom is to break out of the side 1 & 2 mindset and your starting point for switching from one side to the other is simply a deep desire to achieve something. Pursue your true passions and doors will begin to swing open for you.

For those of you who are starting with nothing like I did, I suggest you take an in-depth look at your lifestyle and the kind of person you are, then set out to change your situation. Be open to ideas that you might not normally entertain and understand that changing sides takes time, effort and thought. It may not be easy but it can happen and whatever you do, don't give up. If you expect to succeed you will. Your confident energy and positive impact will be returned to you. So make a decision as to which side of money you want to create your lifestyle from, and know that you can achieve anything in this life because you are in control and you have the power. Remember, you always have two options in life: you can think small and be mediocre or you can be bad and think big.

"BAD BOYS FINISH RICH" – EXERCISE APPENDIX-E

- Which side of money do you derive the most income from today?

- What control do you have on the side of money you are on?

- What are you not in control of?

- Are you comfortable on the side of money that you are on right now?

- Do you feel that you are already on the side of money where you can be successful?

- Which side of money provides the best opportunity for you to make the most money?

69

- Comparing the sides of money, which side will you be on when you reach the pinnacle of your success?

- Are you willing to consider self-education to expand your vision of the four sides of money?

- Are you willing to go through the process of learning how to change from one side of money to the other?

- What are you going to do about it?

FINI$H RICH!

"You are the head, not the tail!"

~ Betty Bolden

Chapter Six

OWN THE TEAM; DON'T JUST PLAY THE GAME

(If you w ant something, all you have
to do is find an asset to pay for it)

In an economy driven more than ever by competition and innovation, the people who succeed tend to be those who thrive on risk and reinvention. Work has become their play and play has become their work. Wealth is a way of thinking not just a dollar amount in the bank. Being rich is not about what you have; it's about who you've chosen to be. If you don't think this way, you will never be rich, no matter how much money you have. The sole purpose of this course is to unleash your economic potential by addressing self-defeating inappropriate behavior patterns that will allow you to re-write your own script and construct your own empowerment. If you want different results or an improved lifestyle, you have to see, think and act differently. You have to psychologically and emotionally elevate yourself to give yourself the grounds to be bold and confident.

As I have previously stated many times throughout this course, the first thing you must do is examine how you see, think and behave regarding matters of wealth and success. Where is your power if you are still just an employee or a customer of a business owned by someone else? Let me help you out, you are non-competitive. Even entrepreneur and basketball great Magic Johnson shared this sentiment when he shared these words with Shaquille O'Neal, "It's ok to be a superstar, to be the man in L.A., but sooner or later you need to start owning things." Don't follow blindly. Regardless of your job, income or education, you have to play to win and playing to win means setting your own course rather than continuing to play a game that's contrary to your own best interest. For the purposes of this course, let's say that true wealth and success begin with owning and controlling your life. With the mind-set of ownership, you will begin to have more control over your destiny.

First, it requires that you make up your mind that you no longer intend to be mediocre. Whether you're from the hood, a rural area or the suburbs, the attitude is surprisingly the same. We tend to see ourselves as only being able to survive rather than thrive. We live in the richest and most capitalistic nation on earth, don't just sit back and accept the status quo. Simply surviving is not the norm. We grow by shedding limitations and by choosing to be more than we are. Your journey from merely surviving to getting rich in all aspects of your life will require a great deal of growing up. And the real benefit of becoming wealthy won't be in the money that's acquired, but in building your self-worth and discovering your personal power. Starting today, look beyond who you are to who you want to be. *BAD BOYS FINI$H RICH* is not only about getting rich, it is about discovering who you really are.

PERSONAL PRESS RELEASES

The rise of new technologies and the free flow of information around the world allow practically anybody, anywhere to make a fortune today with the right idea. Thanks to WordPress anybody anywhere in the world can have a website and blog with a few clicks of a mouse. Facebook and Twitter give you a social community and a public relations   outlet. YouTube allows you to broadcast your own television station so to speak around the world. Built in recording software is at your fingertips on Apple computers and thanks to PayPal, Google Checkout, and Yahoo Small Business, to name a few, you can have an online storefront to accept money. The amount of money flowing around the world is so large that fortunes are being made in areas of the world that most of us have never even heard of. A new breed of rich people are either buying or creating assets. Determining what is and isn't an asset is simple. An asset is something that puts money in your pocket whether you work or not. The key is whether you work or not. There are four main asset classes: Businesses, Real estate, Paper (stocks, bonds, mutual funds) and Commodities (gold, silver, oil, gas, etc.) but, the asset that gives you the greatest control is you. It's not real estate, stocks, hard work or money that makes you rich; it's your attitude about real estate, stocks, hard work and money. The process we go through is even more important than the goal itself because who we become in the process as a result of all the mistakes, learning and experiences, is where the real value lies. The real question is: Are you willing to break free from your self-imposed limitations and own the team not just play the game? You have the capability, but you have assumed that the amount of money that you make or lack thereof is the problem when that's not the real issue. The real problem is nothing more than your attitude, opinion and point of view about who you are and who you want to become. No matter how much you want to be rich, you'll continually be stuck in a state of mediocrity as long as you think your point of view about money is the only way life can be for you. To change what you have, first you have to change your mind about who you are. When you seriously consider that statement, you become your own genie that you let out of the bottle.

THE POSTER CHILD
FOR MY OWN MOVEMENT

Even under the best circumstances, it is no simple task for any of us to come to an understanding of who we are and our relationship to the world. I started from ground zero and put together a plan that literally put the odds in my favor. My goal was simple: "Own the team; don't just play the game." I changed the way that I thought about wealth because my knowledge of how to get rich sucked and I saved myself because no one was coming to save me. I took the attitude that it's not what I had to do, it's who

I chose to become and made getting rich my intention. It's still a daily process but well worth it because I know I am creating a new legacy for my family.

Gandhi said "make a conscious decision to be the change we need to see." Today I'm a serial entrepreneur always looking for a problem to solve and an industry to try to invent. Since I was a little boy, my mom has always motivated me by telling me *"You are the head, not the tail",* and you know what? I believed her. My mom constantly drilled in me to believe in God and to believe in myself and I was raised by a resilient woman who instilled a strong work ethic in me and the expectation that I would succeed regardless of my chosen path. I grew up with total abundance because of my mom's resourcefulness. It amazes me to this day how well she managed with five kids. You make your own way in this world and you can be whoever you want to be. I really feel like I've found what I was meant to do.

IF NOT YOU THEN WHO?

Ownership for me came in the form of intellectual property enabling me to spread my personal philosophy, message and principles of self-reliance. Your life story, your knowledge and your message… what you know from experience and want to share with the world have greater importance and market value than you probably ever dreamed. If you have struggled through something and survived, you should help those now struggling. If you have achieved the impossible, make it possible for others to achieve the same. I share my backstory because I want you to know I have been where you are now. I have struggled to get my message out there, but now I am here to help you. We are in this together. The only question now is whether you care enough about your self-worth, personal growth, self-reliance and financial freedom to overcome your fears. Will you show up? Will you be an employer or an employee? Swiss American psychiatrist

Elisabeth Kubler-Ross views it this way: "When you come to the edge of all the light you know and are about to step into the darkness of the unknown, faith is knowing that one of two things will happen: there will be something solid to stand on, or you'll be taught to fly." Sometimes just having someone tell us that we can raise our standards can be impetus to actually change. You don't know how bad your unconscious is derailing everything you do. Let me explain why I say that. We get to choose what kind of game we play in life in order to be rewarded and recognized. If you've read this far, then you now know more about how to become self- made than I did when I began. You have a great foundation and you have a large head start on the rest of the world.

The takeaway of this chapter is this: *BAD BOYS FINI$H RICH is* the American Dream and the quintessential American Dream is all about financial freedom. If that's your dream too, there's no need to hide your ambition anymore. First, you have to be the one who would just naturally do successful things before you can have what you want. The process is very simple, but if you don't believe in the probability of your success,   you won't make it happen. When you become rich and successful, it will be because of who you are not because of what you have. I challenge you to live a fuller, richer, happier and more meaningful life.

"BAD BOYS FINISH RICH" – EXERCISE APPENDIX-F

Work this exercise backwards! Starting with HAVE, write down everything you want from life that you don't have. Then, write what you would have to DO in order to have what you want. Finally, decide who you would need to BE in order to HAVE what you want. BE = DO = HAVE.

FINI$H RICH!

If you had one shot, or one opportunity to seize everything you ever wanted in one moment, would you capture it or just let it slip?

~Eminem

Chapter Seven

A NEW BREED OF RICH PEOPLE

(Serve more people and give people who have the ambition
the opportunity to live the lifestyle that they desire)

Three percent of Americans are millionaires... the other 97% work to make them even richer. To join the 3 percent, you have to know the secret that the richest people don't want you to know. And the secret is... there are no secrets. There is no Santa Claus, no Tooth Fairy and there is no wizard at the end of the yellow brick road. They are called secrets because the mindset and action required to succeed is largely ignored and not acted upon. So, what this tells you is that the bottom line is, if we want something we can make it happen. All you have to do is take action.

Mansions, exotic cars and private jets... my first action is to say, "I want one of those." Hell, I want all of those. Do you want to take the journey with me to get them? Wait a minute, I didn't ask you if we could afford them or even if we should try to get them. I asked you if you would like to. You see, just like momma always told you, you can do anything if you focus on doing it rather than why you can't. So we're not going to spend any time on why we can't. That has no value. We're going to focus on how we can, but to do so would be virtually impossible according to the standard way of thinking. So, the first thing we have to do is take ourselves to places we never even thought of going through a system of re-education and indoctrination. So what does that mean? It means that the only way you can understand the real meaning and purpose of this course is to be willing to unlearn old behavior models, strategies and learned helplessness and be willing to learn how to play by a new set of rules..."Yours!"

LESSONS OF ECONOMIC
SELF-RELIANCE

My goal is to teach you what to do, say, think and how to act to unravel the great mysteries about wealth and success; to give anyone and everyone the attitude, mind-set and tools to achieve the American Dream. The mere fact that you took the first step by ordering this course leads me to believe that you are willing to go all the way. So what we will do now is turn our attention to principles that you will never learn in any other course. These are the five steps I used to move from angry and frustrated to financially free in a few short years. These five steps helped me find my financial fast track and I continue to use them today. I trust that they can assist you in charting your own course to financial freedom.

Step # 1: It's not what you have to do; it's who you choose to become. I left the military to pursue the Internet along with millions of others. As I said before, I wanted to own the team, not just play the game. My plan was to form a system of distributors to sell my concept nationally and to travel internationally. One of the greatest lessons I've learned is that if you help others get what they want you can get what you want. Just as I am pursuing my dream, I want to help you choose the direction for your life and achieve the quality of life that you desire. You probably know someone like me who has less talent or education than you do, but who doesn't seem to need to work so hard to make a comfortable living. This in itself should be sufficient to convince you that you are capable of the same. There's an anonymous quote that says, "The greatest waste in the world is the difference between who we are and what we could've become." For me, it was about the process of continually wanting to be better, challenging myself to pursue excellence on every level. The question I had to ask myself everyday was: What do I have to do to reach my full potential? My answer was always the same. Be bad or die! I know it sounds dramatic, but I realized that the *BAD BOYS FINI$H RICH* attitude was the vehicle I could use to take the subject of money off the table when it came to deciding what I was going to do in my life and my life changed completely. Being bad has always separated leaders from followers and those who succeed from those who just get by. Within the context of this course, being bad is what creates progress, and progress is what will advance you beyond the competitive herd of the masses, mediocrity and status quo. Don't just sit around wondering what will happen next. Push the envelope and boldly brandish your ambition!

Step # 2: Find something that people have a desire for and provide a solution for that desire. This is where I pull the curtain back on my lifestyle and show you how you can join me. Every problem is a product. Find the problem and sell the solution. The trick is to find a problem that a lot of people have, solve it and sell them the solution. Then you automatically direct people who have that problem to your solution. Then you do it again and again until your passive income allows you to live your dreams. You have that in this course. The truth is deep down everyone wants to be wealthy, live in a mansion, drive exotic cars and travel around the world in private jets. *BAD BOYS FINI$H RICH* is the desire and solution for millions upon millions of people throughout the world. At its heart, this is a course about driving change and making individual, group and systemic progress. It is about being true to yourself at every stage of your journey and identifies the self-defeating patterns of thought that burden so many people today and articulates new approaches that can help you break free to pursue the exciting opportunities of tomorrow.

Step # 3: Take an asset and build a system around it. Most people do not know how to set up businesses like that. I say this to illustrate that this course has taught you how to do that. It's not fate, luck, chance or coincidence you found my message at this point in your life. I believe you are here because deep within you, there is a restlessness stirring to share who you are with the world in a bigger way. My intent is to provide you the means of putting into action the techniques that I have taught you and as you apply these techniques, you will see that others will get the same benefits as you. Building wealth and achieving success shouldn't be about using every last ounce of your own energy and resources to get there, that carries too much personal cost and sometimes can prevent you from achieving success. Therefore, it is imperative that you explore the use of other people's resources in a mutually-beneficial manner. In other words, everybody wins. We all possess the seeds of greatness and *BAD BOYS FINI$H RICH* provides the tools to discover and nourish those seeds. You have the opportunity to stand up and direct others to a greater future for themselves. This is your time to lead and serve. Amidst all the fear and uncertainty in the world, you can be the light that guides the way.

Step # 4: Give as many people who have the ambition an opportunity to live the lifestyle that they desire. My number one job in business is to teach and serve people. I generally want to help others solve their problems and reach their potential. I want to give everyone who reads my books a sense of well-being as well as improved self-confidence and self- esteem. There's no limit to how far or wide the power of the *BAD BOYS FINI$H RICH* principles can reach. Twenty-eight percent of Americans say that once they have paid for their personal expenses, they don't have any extra money. The goal is to help you develop critical thinking skills and develop an actual ability or skill set to achieve a specific outcome. So many people constantly dream of some far-off success. Imagine the life you want and decide to live it. Don't spend years in meaningless existence simply going to work at a boring job you don't like, trying to earn a living and feeling stuck in a career because it's convenient. Don't settle for less than you can be financially. Survival should not be your only option. Take heed to the words of Marianne Williamson from her book *A Return to Love*, "Our deepest fear is that we are powerful beyond measure. It is our light, not our darkness, that most frightens us. We ask ourselves, who am I to be brilliant, gorgeous, talented, and fabulous? Actually, who are you not to be? Your playing small does not serve the world. As we are liberated from our own fear, our presence automatically liberates others." If you have the right attitude, what's in front of you is far more important that what is behind you, and where you are going is more significant than where you came from or where you have been. You have the potential, we all do and you've come to the right course. You are now a student of *"BOLD Ambition"* and you're among friends now so you don't have to keep your secret desire of becoming a millionaire a secret anymore. It's not a sin to crave millions of dollars. It's not a sin to want to be your own boss and build your own business And it's not a sin to want to retire in style. We all want to be millionaires and once you finish this course, I think you'll agree that you're a damn fool if you don't.

Step # 5: It's not about income; it's about assets that generate income. Unless you are independently wealthy, you work to create income. One of the best kept secrets of the wealthy is to leverage the skills and talents of other people. A capitalist's purpose is to make money by synergistically orchestrating other people's money, other people's talents and other people's time, and a true business is a profitable enterprise that will work ideally without you. Think about that, a profitable enterprise that will work 24/7, 365 without you. Most entrepreneurs don't really have a business; they just have another job that creates a lot of stress. The idea of BOLD Ambition and *BAD BOYS FINI$H RICH* is to become a business owner where you have an organization or business that will work without you having to be there and it would still bring in a passive income. That's money while you sleep if you are interested. Now let's be honest, to do that, you will need to leverage other people's money, other people's talents and other people's time. Depending on the income you desire and the commitment that you make to building your business, once you have grown your organization of like-minded individuals and everyone is working together in alignment as entrepreneurs (virtual assistants and outsourced contractors), you can reduce the time that you put in and enjoy the fruits of your labor. Of course the ultimate question is how does this all apply to you? The era of ask and you shall receive is dead. *BAD BOYS who FINI$H RICH* live and breathe by the credo, "Go get it and you shall receive." Unlocking that door simply comes by altering your pattern of thought. I understand where you are, I've been there and I have developed a system that allows me to follow my dreams and at the same time try make all the money I want to make. I make it my business to provide opportunities so for those of you who have decided to use the *BAD BOYS FINI$H RICH* principles I offer the following advice: "DON'T FIND A JOB, CREATE ONE!" Now I know that the mere imparting of this statement is not education. Above all, my screaming it at you must result in making you think and do for yourself, so let me show you a very simple plan that can allow you to earn a very significant income and build a very lucrative business.

FIVE STEPS TO A BAD BOYS FINI$H RICH EMPIRE

I.   Create a low-priced information product: An Information product is basically training material of your advice or strategies for success packaged into an educational product or program typically in the price range of $20-$200.

II.   Create a low-priced subscription program: Deliver content to your customers in a continuity program or membership program just like the magazine business model by sending monthly content to them in the form of a training video or by hosting a training call over a conference call line which gives them more training or answers questions. To access the video and the call replays, your customers will login to a members-only site and download the video or audio recordings.

III.   Create a mid-tier-priced information product: A more advanced and comprehensive training program such as a $497 DVD home study course on your topic. The home study course could include 10 DVDs, transcripts, a workbook and a bonus 3-disc audio program.

IV.   Create a high-tier multi-day seminar: Customers are interested in mastery and continuing their education. If they bought your book, audio and DVD programs, now they want to go deeper and learn from you live.

V.   Create a high-priced coaching program: Customers want your personal attention. They want you to assess their needs and work with them to develop a plan to move them closer towards their dream.

Because you can reach so many people and share information and digital products so inexpensively with the worldwide activity of the Internet this exact moment constitutes one of the greatest entrepreneurial opportunities in history. Let me show you the numbers. If you created a $197 information product and sold just one product a day for 30 days, you would earn $5,910 a month. If you do the math, this product can make you over $70,000 a year. If you get just 100 people to pay you $97 a month for your subscription program you would be earning an extra $9,700 a month. Multiply that by 12 and your 100 clients are paying you a little over $116,000 per year. If you sold just two a day of your $497 DVD home study course you would earn $29,820 a month and $357,840 a year. Can you see how fast this can all add up?

If any of this sounds unbelievable, then it's because far too many of us are naïve and shortsighted in regard to our innate power that can be multiplied and increased beyond measure. Set your sights high and believe in your potential and a grand destiny for yourself. People pay a lot of money to shorten their learning curve and their path to success. They are looking for specific information that helps them solve their problems, whether personal or professional and move ahead faster in life. I teach my skill-set which is self-reliance, but it's critical for you to tell your story from your perspective. You can get paid for sharing advice and how-to information that helps others succeed and with the advent of print on demand manufacturing and distribution, the first three steps are a clear business model for new entrepreneurs who want a business that generates thousands of dollars a month on an automated, recurring basis with little work on your part.

"BAD BOYS FINISH RICH" – EXERCISE APPENDIX-G

The entire *BAD BOYS FINI$H RICH* brand was built on my internal struggle to free myself and be self-reliant and to help others who feel stuck or trapped and don't know how or have a clue where to start.   Answer the following questions to discover your own product topics and ideas.

- What have you learned about managing money?
- What have you learned about motivating yourself and achieving your dreams?

- What have you learned about business or entrepreneurship?

- What have you learned about spirituality or connecting with a higher power?

- What have you learned about being in a relationship?

- What have you learned about decorating or fashion?

- What have you learned about marketing a product?

- What have you learned about balancing your life?

BUILD YOUR EMPIRE
ON YOUR OWN TERMS

You have an amazing chance to absorb the lessons from this course. You'll never have that mansion and the freedom that wealth brings if you aim to survive instead of thrive. The moral of the story is this: If you're not involved, you're not playing the game, and if you're not playing the game, you can't possibly win. You have taken the world's most dangerous life and entrepreneurship course. Dangerous because it showed you how to break free and own and control your own life: A life of freedom where you do what you want, when you want, wherever you want. This is not an exaggeration. It's the truth. This course is dangerous because it has shifted the balance of power and put your destiny in your hands. However you define the word rich, with the information in this course, you can become rich: Rich in money, Rich in freedom, Rich in possibilities. This course gave you the information; how you use it is up to you. My research and years of experience tell me that what we really need to do to succeed at the highest level is to think differently. The new rules within this course will help you do just that. The journey is internal so let me remind you that, if you can't create your own opportunity, it's because you are playing by the rules and believing that you are who society told you you are supposed to be. I vowed that I would never let that fate become mine. I determined never to settle. I will never accept a life of mediocrity and I will never work for others. I will be my own man. No fears will intimidate me, no critics can make me doubt myself and I will never depend on anyone. I will be free, independent and in control of my own life. If you are afraid to fail, I suggest that you stop reading close this course and go back to living a mediocre life and living within the status quo, but understand that the decisions you make can alter your life forever. If you follow the instructions outlined in this course, the results will be automatic and you'll realize that you are capable of achieving, earning and possessing far more than you ever thought possible. Somewhere in this course, I hope you have recognized yourself because something important awaits you beyond financial freedom. I feel honored that our paths have crossed and that I've been able to share with you what I've learned, but it is a life-long process and I'm still learning. Sometimes, I told myself, "You have no experience and you didn't even graduate from college. You don't have a chance, stop wasting your time. Looking back, this was one of my low points, but definitely not the only one of my long journey. It was one of the many occasions when I came close to deciding to give up my dream. I didn't have a dime in the bank and my personal debts were approaching $150,000. However, each time that I considered giving up, some small victory materialized to keep me going. I hoped and prayed and trudged forward. Despite setback after setback, I stayed in the game. It gave me a boost of confidence and convinced me that my goal was within reach. Looking back, I was a married man with a family and a dream. I had high hopes, lots of energy and unbridled enthusiasm. I was implementing the plan that has made my dream an attainable goal. There have been obstacles to overcome every step of the way, and a lot of looking in the mirror for encouragement, but, I knew that if I just didn't give up, I could make it happen. I was in constant motion and things were happening. It was the most exciting time in my life and I don't think I've ever had more fun. There was a method to my madness. Can you imagine? A poor kid from Tampa developed the philosophy that today creates owners and develops millionaires. My crazy dream is now my life. I proved all the critics wrong.

Now that you know a little about my story and my dream I hope that in writing *BAD BOYS FINI$H RICH*, I have become part of your story and I hope you've been inspired to share your own voice and that you continue to do so for life. Andrew Carnegie said "There is power under your control that is greater than poverty, greater than the lack of education, greater than all of your fears and superstitions combined." All you have to do is decide if this is the right calling and opportunity for you or not. This is your time. Be bad and make a difference and it will happen because you will refuse to allow circumstances to remain the same. So my final thought is to share the words of NC State coach Jim Valvano: "If I can get you to see what I'm seeing and to dream what I'm dreaming, we can get there!" Join me on the journey of a lifetime.

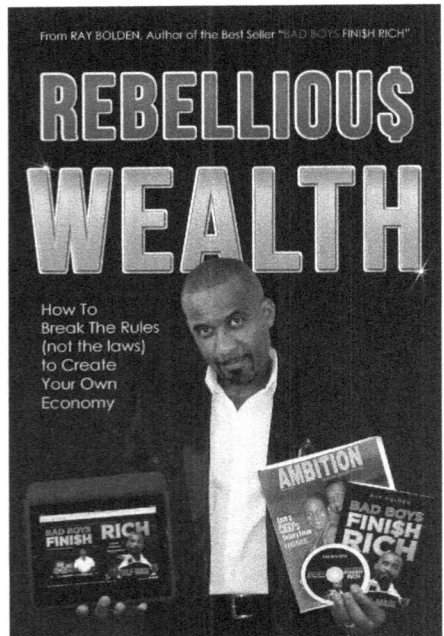

BAD BOYS FINISH RICH
AFFILIATE PROGRAM

Earn $5.00 - $10.00 Per Sale

For Every Customer You Refer!

BE BAD
WITH THE NEW GENERATION
CEO & BEST SELLING AUTHOR

Visit **BADBOYSFINISHRICH.COM/bebad** and become an Affiliate today!

FOLLOW RAY ON SOCIAL MEDIA

**PERSPECTIVES ON FINANCIAL LITERACY AND ENTREPRENEURIAL
EDUCATION THAT OFTEN CONTRADICT CONVENTIONAL WISDOM**

Follow Ray on Facebook:

www.facebook.com/boldambitionworldwide

Follow Ray on Twitter:

www.twitter.com/IamMrBolden

Follow Ray on Amazon:

www.amazon.com/Ray-Bolden/e/B00VXC3YN4/ref=ntt_dp_epwbk_0

Please Note: After enjoying Ray's work, please provide a customer review
and give feedback on Amazon.com.

Visit **BADBOYSFINISHRICH.COM/about_ray**

BAD BOYS FINISH RICH

BOLD AMBITION
WORLDWIDE

www.ingramcontent.com/pod-product-compliance
Lightning Source LLC
Chambersburg PA
CBHW071111210326
41519CB00020B/6264